The Elements of Clear Thinking

Accurate Communication

William F. McCart

Educators Publishing Service, Inc.
31 Smith Place
Cambridge, MA 02138-1000

Contents

Cover Design by Joyce Weston

Educators Publishing Service, Inc.
31 Smith Place, Cambridge, MA 02138

 ISBN 0-8388-0167-6 Printed in the U.S.A.

February 2000 Printing

Introduction

A movie recently shown on television told the story of a creature from another planet who came to earth to help human beings. He assumed human form and knew our language, but did not use words to express his ideas as we do. Instead, he resorted to his supernatural ability to read minds and to send and receive thoughts directly. The people he tried to help were confused and frightened by this power and he was not able to solve their problems. They needed words to exchange ideas. Without words they could not reach understanding.

We can communicate some things without using words—with gestures, facial expressions, body language, even by our dress and walk, but complicated thoughts can be expressed and understood only with *words*—particular combinations of letters and their sounds which we all agree will stand for the objects we live with and the concepts we house in our minds. The purpose of this book is to help you to develop greater skill in the communication of ideas—to do so accurately with the only means we have available: spoken and written words.

Meaning cannot be communicated literally. Words and messages can be sent and received, but their meaning comes clear only after the words have stimulated our thinking. I may, for instance, know the meaning of all the words you use, but if I don't understand how and why you used them in a particular way I will not get your meaning. The misunderstanding, confusion, and frustration we cause each other come about either because we don't send clear messages or because we don't listen and read carefully enough to grasp the meaning.

In the informal communicating we do at home and with friends, misunderstanding can be quickly corrected. We can repeat or clarify the message. There are fewer chances to correct poor communication in the classroom. An incorrect response to a teacher, a misunderstood chapter in a book, or even a misplaced check mark on a test all work against our success. Learning demands accurate communication. Clear thinking is possible only when we listen and read carefully enough to grasp the meaning which the sender intended to communicate.

1

Clear Thinking Begins with Choosing the Right Words

The problem we face with words is that they don't mean anything in themselves. They are only sounds and markings. They become useful to us only because we have all agreed that they will stand for an object or an idea. It would be foolish to ask a baby to pass you the salt, but it would be equally foolish to ask someone who knows nothing about chemistry to pass you the sodium chloride. We have to learn the sounds and the letters and what they stand for before we can think and act in response.

These spoken and written symbols have a life of their own. They are created as names for new things and new ideas when needed. They can change and come to mean different things as we use them. For example, the word *candid* means "frank, straightforward." Yet many students on tests now give the word *hidden* as a synonym. The reason for this may be that millions of people watched the television program Candid Camera, in which a microphone and camera were concealed to record people unaware in comical situations. In time the word *candid* could come to mean the exact opposite; not "frank and open" but "hidden, concealed." Words also die out, become archaic or obsolete, because the objects they stand for no longer exist or the ideas they represent are no longer popular.

The first step toward communicating accurately is to recognize the need to be precise in selecting words and to be clear about the meaning of the words you hear and read. Words are not frozen in their meanings, like ice; they're more like flowing water.

A dictionary is the most authoritative source we can use in our search for precise meaning. In addition to providing us with definitions, a good dictionary will give us other words with meanings similar to the word in question, will supply examples in which the various meanings of the word are to be used appropriately, and will tell us the origin of the word so that we can see how the different meanings evolved. Even with all this help, however, the ultimate meaning of the word and the sense it makes will come from the way the author uses it in the context of his sentence and the purpose he had in choosing it for his particular reasons.

We have thousands of words at our command which we can use for our everyday exchanges with people. We have thousands more available to us because we recognize them and know what they mean when we encounter them in reading and listening to lectures and speeches. We keep increasing this reserve of recognizable words as we read and listen more extensively and incorporate new words into our speech and writing. The need for precision in our understanding and use of these words becomes more important as we increase and expand our ideas, express ourselves more fully, and attempt to deal with complex matters. In all of this developing process the key to communicating accurately remains with the selection of the right word, used in the appropriate context, and serving its intended purpose.

When you speak or write your choice of words, your purpose is clear to you. You know where you want to lead others to reach your meaning. But hearing or reading other people's words is like finding your way through a forest. The path to an author's meaning is often difficult because you must follow his choice of words, his arrangement of them, and his purpose.

To become skillful in grasping the meaning of countless ideas presented to you in lectures and reading assignments requires that you become aggressive in your attitude toward communicating. It's easy to hear and read the symbols, the words, to understand what is being said. It requires only attention. The hard work lies in searching for the intended meaning of the words. Some people, and especially some students, are very skillful at remembering and repeating exactly what they have heard or read. They usually do very well answering objective test questions such as multiple choice, matching words in columns, or filling in a missing word. But, they are frequently at a loss when they must answer essay questions which require them to explain an author's thoughts in their own words, or to use the author's thoughts as a basis for their own. Real communication, and learning, take place only when you are willing to deal with what we may describe as a verbal invasion. If you are armed with an understanding of exactly what has been said and what was meant, you will be able to accept or reject ideas based on your own good sense, not solely on the persuasive powers of the speaker or the writer.

A. The Variety and Power of Words

If words have lives of their own, then they also have their own personalities. Like people, they can be honest or deceitful, exciting or dull, thoughtful or careless, according to the way we use them. We have a vast supply of words in our language because English has borrowed extensively from many other languages and cultures. This variety and liveliness in English words enables us to discuss very complicated and very subtle ideas with ease—*if* we choose our words carefully. There are dangers, however, for those who are unaware of the many "personalities" contained in the words we use.

The thousands of technical words we learn in subjects like chemistry, physics, biology, and mathematics usually have very specific meanings. There is no doubt about their use because they designate a particular substance or process. Communication in these scientific areas must be very precise. This is not true of more commonly used words and expressions which we employ to convey our opinions and feelings. We have many synonyms for the words used in everyday communication, but although they are all related to the same object or idea, some of them say more to us than others. For instance, you would have a different reaction to what was said and who said it if you were told, "That cur of yours looks starved" rather than, "Your dog looks hungry." The meaning is the same in the two sentences, but the choice of words and the way they are used produce two very different messages. If you have ever been homesick, you know the difference between the words *house, dormitory, hotel,* or any other place to live, and the word *home*. Words do more than designate objects and ideas: they also stir up emotions, positive and negative, and carry our opinions about things and people along with them. They can push and pull our thoughts in many directions.

Conversation and reading would be very dull if the only words we encountered were strictly neutral, that is, devoid of any meaning other than the designated name of the object. It would be like seeing only the colors black and white. There would be no opportunity to enjoy warm, rich shades of red, or cool, subtle shades of green. The variety and different shades of meaning which words can impart clarify and stimulate meaning. The danger lies in not being alert to the impact on our thinking which the different meanings can have. It is not difficult for a skillful speaker or writer to direct our thinking away from what is logical and reasonable towards unfounded, prejudiced, or erroneous conclusions. Our ability to think clearly for ourselves is impaired if we are unaware of other people's choice of words.

Exercise I—Shades of Meaning

In the example given above the dog owner whose pet was referred to as a cur might understandably resent the choice of words. *Cur* is a term of contempt meaning "a mongrel or inferior dog." What other words could the speaker have used? *Canine*? That is a formal, scientific word. *Mongrel*? That tells us that a dog is of unknown or mixed breed. *Mutt*? That also means of mixed origin, but the word is often used as a friendly way to indicate that the dog is not purebred. *Pup* or *doggie* would describe a young or small dog. *Beast* would suggest a big, perhaps frightening animal, less a pet than a working dog.

To appreciate the shades of meaning which different words can suggest to us, read the words on each of the lines below. The words are names of things or they are adjectives which describe things. Each group includes a word which is neutral; that is, it names the object or describes it as it is with no overtones of either positive or negative feelings or suggestions. *Circle* the words which you consider neutral. *Underline once* the words which you think have positive overtones. *Underline twice* the words which have negative overtones. Think of these terms as applying to yourself, a friend, and someone or something you don't like.

1. clever intelligent shrewd smart wise cunning bright
2. runt little small tiny shrimp diminutive petite
3. residence domicile house abode home apartment tenement
4. angry furious mad crazy annoyed incensed
5. cop police officer officer law enforcement officer pig
6. fat obese gross plump heavy
7. slim skinny thin slender
8. writer hack scribbler author
9. stupid dull dumb unintelligent slow dim not bright
10. public servant political hack political boss ward-heeler politician
11. old elderly ancient decrepit aged mature
12. brat youth young adult teen-ager
13. frantic upset excited nervous tense
14. lawyer attorney shyster counselor mouthpiece
15. argument battle discussion disagreement fight difference of opinion

Exercise II—The Negative Slant

Rewrite each of the sentences below to change the factual statement given into one which conveys negative feelings about the person or the act.

EXAMPLE

The governor pardoned the prisoner.

The governor let the criminal go free.

1. The instructor lectured for the class period.

___

___

2. The soccer team lost the game on Saturday.

3. The party at Sally's last week was quiet.

4. When the new tax law goes into effect next month we will all have to pay an additional three percent sales tax.

5. The crowd at the arena became very excited when the band started to play.

Exercise III—The Positive Slant

Rewrite each of the statements below to change the negative feelings which some of the words evoke into positive feelings about the person or the act.

EXAMPLE

The soccer team was slaughtered on Saturday.

In spite of the great effort made by the soccer team on Saturday, the visiting team prevailed.

1. The only reason he won the election is that he used every trick in the book.

2. The taxpayers of this city are fed up with being saddled with heavy tax increases every couple of years, and they're going to throw the mayor and his political cronies out of office in the next election.

3. He's too dumb to get into that Ivy League college.

4. The mob was going wild and the cops charged through the street, shoving back anyone who broke through the line.

5. For a little freshman he's got a big mouth when he's talking to seniors on the Student Council.

____

____

Choosing one word over another, selecting a neutral word or one with positive or negative overtones to express your meaning, will produce different reactions from different people. You must be sensitive to the effect your choice will have because words can make us happy or miserable. They can start wars or end them; elect leaders or ruin careers. Words can rule us—or we can rule them. The critical point in communication begins when you take care to make your meaning clear and do not confuse or distract people with meanings you did not intend to convey.

B. Deceptive Words

There are two kinds of words which create confusion and block clear thinking between the sender and the receiver: one is ambiguous words, and the other is vague words.

Ambiguous means that the word used could be understood in more than one sense or meaning. Because many words have several different meanings, we can mistake the meaning we have in mind with the one the speaker intended. For instance, a dictionary may list eleven different meanings for the word *free.* In one sense it means "determined by one's own wishes," as in *free actions.* In another sense it means "without cost," like *a free ticket,* and in another sense it may mean "not dominated by others," as in *a free citizen.* If someone stated his opinion in the sentence *Public colleges and universities should be free,* he could mean either that such colleges should not impose any restrictions on the students who go there or seek admission, or that they should not charge students any fees to attend them, or perhaps that no external power such as a state government should control them.

The only way that you would know which of these meanings the speaker intended is if you asked "Free from what?" or "Free for whom?" It is not uncommon for people to carry on an argument and never reach any conclusions because they never clarified the sense or meaning of an ambiguous word. To keep your thinking clear, therefore, you have to eliminate the ambiguity first. If you are following a speaker or writer carefully, you will recognize the possible differences in meaning which some of his words may have. The next step is to pin down the specific sense in which the word is being used. Watch closely. Some people slip in two different meanings in the same discussion in order to trap you. For instance, consider the following:

"I think competition is a healthful thing in our society. It's what keeps prices down and quality up in all the products we buy. So it's a good thing to have competition in the classroom too. It keeps students on their toes."

In the first instance competition implies that one company is offering a cheaper price or better quality in order to beat its rival. But, in the second instance, competition means trying to be as good as or better than other members of a group. The aim of competition in business is to sell products. The aim of competition among people is to achieve a personal goal. Shifting the meaning confuses the point of the argument.

It is the words we use commonly to express feelings and opinions which are more apt to be used ambiguously. Words like *equal, freedom, trust, love, religion, democracy, cooperation, fair, honest,* and many others which stand for important concepts in our lives can have almost as many meanings as the number of people using them. Be sure that you and the speaker or you and the author have the same meaning in mind. Words are not ambiguous in themselves; we make them ambiguous by the way we use them.

Exercise IV—Spotting Ambiguity

In each of the sentences below a word is used ambiguously. Underline the ambiguous word each time it is used. Then, after consulting a dictionary, write two different meanings which the word has in different contexts.

1. In a democracy everyone should be free, so I should be free to live the way I want to without being hassled by the government.

   1. ______________________________

   2. ______________________________

2. I was brought up to believe that honesty is the best policy. When I told Barbara that the food she served at her party was rotten, I was only being honest.

   1. ______________________________

   2. ______________________________

3. The only way to get along with people is to cooperate with them. When I gave Ramon the answer to the last question on the exam we were only cooperating for our mutual success.

   1. ______________________________

   2. ______________________________

4. The Declaration of Independence says that we are all created equal, so it isn't fair to make people take an entrance exam for a state university. We should all have an equal chance to go there.

   1. ______________________________

   2. ______________________________

5. I don't agree with the radical changes the City Council wants to make in the way this city is run. Too many radicals will destroy the town.

   1. ______________________________

   2. ______________________________

The second kind of deceptive word which acts to block clear thinking is the vague word. Such words as *tall, heavy, fast, liberal, young, old, good, bad,* and many more like them stand for a quality which a thing may have. The problem with such words is that we are not always precise about how much of the quality a thing must have in order to be thus characterized. For instance, up to what age can we say that someone is young? Twenty? Thirty? When can we say that a person is old? Forty? Sixty? Eighty? If we say that a person has liberal ideas, we must have some idea of how liberal, or in what ways the person is liberal, before we can agree that those qualities are being properly described by the word *liberal.*

Vague words, on the other hand, can be very useful. We use them all the time as a kind of conversational shorthand. Rather than saying, "The temperature today is 92 degrees," we usually say, "It's hot today." We say someone is rich, or very rich, or poor, or very poor, without giving our cut-off point for what we think of as being rich or poor. Attempting to be exact about the degree of every quality we describe in everyday conversation would make discussion ponderous and boring. We all have a general idea of when the word is appropriately used.

There are times, nevertheless, when we have to be precise about the degree of the quality we describe. To say that someone is short will not be precise enough if the person is trying to qualify for a job which sets a minimum standard of height for the job. When a school has a policy of passing students in a course who have gotten a sixty on the final exam, then fifty-nine is failing. It isn't enough to use terms like *poor students* or *weak grades*; the cut-off point has been determined to avoid vague interpretations of the words *passing* and *failing*.

Our difficulty with vague words arises when we use them in an either-or, or all-or-nothing manner. If people think that something is either good or bad, dangerous or harmless, and use these words to indicate that in their minds there are no differences in the degree of goodness or badness, danger or harm, they are giving the word a fixed meaning which it does not have. They will not admit any gradation from all good to all bad, or any differences between extremely dangerous to completely harmless. Since people, things, and events in our lives rarely fall into only two separate categories with no place in between, individuals who force vague words into a fixed position do not argue logically and create confusion in our thinking.

To eliminate ambiguous meanings which can get us off the track of clear thinking, we saw that we must pin down the particular meaning the author had in mind when using a word. To eliminate the confusion which vague words can create, we have to gauge to what extent the quality described applies. We have to ask questions like, "How much?" "To what extent?" and "What kind do you mean?"

Exercise V—Clarifying Vague Words

In the sentences below underline any vague words which you think would need clarification before you could understand the author and agree or disagree with the statement. On the lines below each sentence write the questions which you would ask the author in order to establish a more precise meaning of the word.

1. The rich should be taxed much more heavily than the poor.

   ____

   ____

2. Only really smart people should be elected to government office. We need the best brains we can get to run the country.

   ____

   ____

3. We're in a bad situation. I don't see any way out of it.

   ____

   ____

4. I'm as liberal as anyone else, but I can't see letting foreigners flood into this country unchecked.

   ____

   ____

5. It's the best shampoo on the market. It's really good for your hair.

   ____

   ____

In this chapter we have examined the use of three kinds of words; emotive words which evoke feelings about the object named beyond the neutral meaning of the word, ambiguous words which can create doubt by having more than one meaning, and vague words which have to be clarified to be meaningful. The exercise below asks you to identify each of these kinds of words.

Exercise VI—Getting the Precise Meaning

Read each sentence carefully and identify the kind of word used by placing the letter *E* for emotive, *A* for ambiguous, or *V* for vague above the word. Then, on the lines below each sentence, rewrite the sentence to change emotive words to more neutral ones, ambiguous words to words or phrases which clearly show the meaning intended in the sentence, vague words to more precise words.

EXAMPLE

We know he was responsible [A] for the slaughter [E] because neighbors [V] saw him do it, but he won't have to go to jail because the law says that if he was insane at the time he wasn't responsible [A] for his actions.

We know he committed the murder (has to take the blame for it) because witnesses saw him do it, but he won't have to go to jail because the law says that if he was insane at the time he cannot be held accountable for his actions (be legally responsible).

1. It was a rotten party, and all the best people left early.

2. Where does he get the right to make us work so hard? We have rights, too.

3. If everyone were free there wouldn't be any riots.

4. That runt on the other team is a great runner.

5. The committee isn't suggesting that we do anything unusual.

6. I know she's bright, but why does she have to act so snobbish?

7. His uncle is a shrewd operator.

8. I don't have a problem with English, but I sure have problems in math.

9. He was just in the wrong place at the wrong time.

10. He says handguns are murder weapons.

11. They made him emperor because he promised them freedom.

12. All we want is our fair share of the profits.

13. It's such a small point; why argue about it?

14. I believe in the United Nations, but I don't believe what our ambassador said at the last meeting of the Security Council.

15. It's a good car. You should buy it.

2

Words Show Feelings

In Chapter One we encountered many words which reflected feelings. Because we aren't computers which have no emotions, our feelings will always affect our thinking to some degree—we simply can't avoid it. When we are trying to make a decision, to choose between two courses of action, or when someone is trying to persuade us to do something or to convince us of something, our emotions are usually aroused. Our feelings will influence our thinking just as our thinking will stir up our feelings. To be able to think clearly, to make decisions based on facts, and to accept an idea as something we will believe and act on, we must be careful to distinguish between thinking and feeling, and attempt to minimize the affect those feelings have on our ability to think logically.

It's easy to keep our thinking clear when we are studying math or science. We are dealing with numbers, chemicals, or organisms usually in a very impersonal way. When we read social studies, literature, or anything to do with people and what happens to them, we are more likely to be personally involved because we tend to identify with the people or situations. The more interesting the story is to us, the more we enter into the world of the feelings of the characters.

In English class you probably learned the difference between the denotation and the connotation of a word. The denotation is the simple, literal definition of the word which you find in a dictionary. The connotation is an additional meaning apart from the denotation. It is what the word suggests as well as what it means. For example, in the first three exercises in Part 1 you were asked to distinguish between the positive and the negative feelings which certain words evoked in contrast to the more neutral word for the same object or quality. You reacted differently to different synonyms for the same things—house-home, dog-cur, big-gross, intelligent-shrewd. A dictionary gave you the synonyms for a particular word which included many words referring to the same object or quality. It did not, however, give you all the meanings suggested by each synonym. If you looked up the word *stubborn,* the synonyms given might include *determined, resolute, unbending, unyielding, obstinate, mulish* and *pig-headed.*

Consider the following three sentences: "We are determined." "You are obstinate." "They are pig-headed." Each adjective in the sentences generally means "remaining fixed, not yielding easily." But there is a wide difference of meaning in each of the sentences because of the connotation each adjective carries. To be determined suggests an admirable quality. Being obstinate suggests not yielding to reason, and pig-headed suggests being perverse or stupidly obstinate. Obviously, from what we know about people who are determined, those who are obstinate, and those who are pig-headed, we are conveying a different level of meaning in each sentence. The connotation of a word gives us the characteristics of the word, what we called its personality in the first chapter.

The varied meanings which synonyms may suggest enrich our language, make it more colorful, more exciting, and provide a more exact vehicle to convey the particular message we mean to give in a communication. What is implied in the connotations we select can give additional information and add a new dimension to the communication. For example, if we refer to a person who is widely known and talked about because of his association with criminals and criminal activities we are sending a more exact message if we refer to him as notorious, rather than famous. We are saying that we know he is more than just famous; he is famous in an unfavorable sense.

We have expressed our opinion of him in choosing *notorious,* with its negative connotation, over *famous,* with its positive connotation. Our choice of words here, however, adds a level of meaning which a listener may think is unfair; that is, the listener may object to our suggesting that a person is somehow guilty because of the people he associates with.

Levels of language can range from the flat, concrete words of a proposition in geometry or computer data to the words of a thrilling novel or movie which can evoke strong emotions. What the level means to us is determined by the words the writer uses, how familiar we are with them, and how carefully we examine the author's use (or misuse) of those words. To understand fully what you hear and read you must grasp all the levels of meaning which a speaker or an author is sending out in his words.

A. Slanted Language

Understanding the full meaning of a statement or an argument can often be more complicated than it seems. The different meanings which the words suggest to us may be used to give an impression that is either favorable or unfavorable to the person or the idea under discussion. This impression can also be achieved by either leaving out important pieces of information or by introducing suggestions that are not pertinent to the issue. This special use of words is called slanting. It can result in clouding over what is true about a person or an issue and leading us to a false or misleading conclusion.

Read the two columns of words below. The words on the left are neutral because they designate or describe something without hinting at either a favorable or unfavorable suggestion. The words on the right suggest more than the neutral words but are synonyms for them which could be used to slant their meaning in another way.

stated	confessed
plan	plot
lie	fib
lie	misstatement
lie	deception
funny	ridiculous
generous	magnanimous
generous	extravagant
complaining	whining
unpleasant	obnoxious
aggressive	energetic
anger	rage
average	mediocre
used	second-hand
used	antique
unhealthful	poisonous
proud	arrogant
be sociable	fraternize
mistake	oversight
mistake	blunder

Using slanted language in behalf of or against a person or situation leaves an impression which may be neither completely true nor completely untrue. What is true will appear only after we have uncovered the bias in the writing by analyzing the author's choice of words. What we want is an unmistakable understanding of the facts, not someone else's interpretation of them.

Exercise I—Slanting the News I

Read the passages below. They were assembled from news items in *Time* magazine about two United States presidents, Harry Truman (33rd pres. 1945-1953), and Dwight Eisenhower (34th pres. 1953-1961). The news items are about the same topics for each president; that is, friends, speeches, taxes, travel, programs, and re-election plans. Read the passages a second time and underline any words or phrases which you consider evidence of slanted language.

Friends

Time, Jan. 28, 1946: "Last week . . . the President eased his croniest crony, George E. Allen, into the Board of Directors of the Reconstruction Finance Corporation." And on Aug. 12, 1946: "George is all the more remarkable because, to the naked eye, he is a clown."

Time, Dec. 14, 1954: "Last week . . . the President chatted quietly with . . . golfing companion George E. Allen, Washington lawyer and friend of Presidents."

Speeches

Time, Jan. 21, 1952: "Pres. Truman flapped open his leather notebook and began in his usual flat tone to read his message to Congress on the State of the Union. When he finished 45 minutes later, he had made little news."

Time, Jan. 17, 1955: "Pres. Eisenhower's 1955 State of the Union speech had sweep and calm balance [and although] it elaborated the obvious, perhaps that was precisely what the nation needed."

Taxes

Time, Mar. 10, 1952: "This week once again, the American taxpayer . . . was working over his income-tax return. He did not do the job happily . . . The blow, in full and crushing measure, now lands each Mar. 15 on the chin of a fellow named John Q."

Time, Apr. 18, 1955: ". . . 60 million Americans have by this week signed their 1954 income-tax forms . . . They did this, wonderful to tell, without riots or protest . . . It has become more and more unfashionable to criticize the income-tax level."

Travel

Time, Mar. 20, 1950: "About May 1, after a month back at his desk in the White House, President Truman will begin a slow trip westward . . . Officially, the trip will be billed as non-political, an ancient device whereby a President can pay his expenses from his $40,000 travel allowance instead of from the party treasury."

Time, June 13, 1955: "From time to time, the President of the United States must travel around the country . . . Last week, Pres. Eisenhower announced one of the most intensive tours since he assumed office . . . University Park, Pa. . . . Washington . . . San Francisco . . . and a speaking tour of Maine, New Hampshire and Vermont."

Programs

Time, May 22, 1950: "In this best of all Democratic worlds he [Truman] had something for everybody. For the businessman, he had his new program of government loan insurance and other aids to small business. For the farmer and consumer, he had the Brannan Plan." And on Jan. 18, 1948: "For everyone else, there was a whole grab-bag of social and economic promises."

Time, Jan. 18, 1954: "Through the departmentalized details of his [Eisenhower's] proposals runs a clear, consistent thread, joining each fact and each measure with all the others. The thread is the general good. He has not thrown together a hodge-podge of group interests. Every proposal seems to be tested by the standard of the whole nation's interest."

Re-election Plans

Time, July 23, 1951: "The subject of Harry Truman's 1952 intentions came up again in his weekly press conference. The President wasn't saying, just acting deliberately mysterious. It has become an unprofitable inquiry and a stale joke."

Time, Jan. 24, 1955: ". . . he [Eisenhower] has skillfully refused to commit himself on 1956." March 14, 1955: "At the President's news conference last week, his 1956 intentions seemed to be on the mind of almost every one of 188 reporters present . . . both the questioners and the answerer were obviously enjoying the banter."

Exercise II—Slanting the News II

The twelve passages in Exercise I are arranged according to the date the news item appeared in *Time* magazine. Beginning with an item about President Truman, the passages alternate from an item about him to a news account about President Eisenhower. Six areas are mentioned; friends, speeches, taxes, travel, programs, and re-election plans. On the lines below, write the words or phrases which *Time* magazine used to slant the news items about these areas, first, negatively *against* President Truman, second, positively *for* President Eisenhower.

EXAMPLES

Friends: Truman croniest crony, clown

Eisenhower golfing companion, friend of Presidents

Speeches: Truman flapped open, flat tone, little news

Eisenhower sweep and calm balance, elaborated the obvious, precisely what the nation needed

Taxes: Truman ______________________

Eisenhower ______________________

Travel: Truman ______________________

Eisenhower ______________________

Programs: Truman ______________________

Eisenhower ______________________

Re-election: Truman ______________________

Eisenhower ______________________

Exercise III—Neutralizing Slanted Language

Each of the ten sentences below contains slanted language. Underline the words or phrases which you consider slanted. Then, rewrite the sentence to remove the negative or positive impression which the slanting gives. Your new sentence should be a neutral presentation.

EXAMPLE

The recent flood of illegal aliens entering our state will rob honest American workers of their jobs.

The increase in the number of illegal aliens who have entered our state may result in fewer jobs being available for legal residents.

1. Senator Smith's vote killed any chance the bill had of passing.

2. He confessed that he was at the scene of the crime earlier that day.

3. Of course she's terrific looking, but she doesn't seem like a real person to me. I don't like girls to be so mysterious.

4. The Student Council is broke because the president squandered money on schemes to beef up the treasury.

5. Jack's got a lot on the ball. He's busy all the time. Where would you find a better candidate?

6. Congress is trying to shove another tax increase down our throats.

7. New, imported HI-GLO face cream now puts glamour within reach of American women.

8. The union leaders stomped out of the meeting, leaving the members of the committee visibly shaken by their abrupt departure.

9. If that bunch of free-spending politicians have their way they'll send the economy crashing down on our heads.

10. He has more guts than I gave him credit for. I swear he must have nearly killed himself to make that run.

It is important to point out that a speaker or a writer may not be using slanted language deliberately. Sometimes, his own views and prejudices come through in his choice of words without his being aware of the impression they will leave. Because we think and feel simultaneously about a person or thing, it is very difficult to express ourselves always in an unemotional manner, using only neutral words. For example, a scientist examining a specimen under a microscope, trying to be as objective as possible, has to be aware that his desire to find exactly what he is looking for to prove a theory, may influence what he sees and records. Because we screen everything we hear and read through a filter of our own opinions about things, clear thinking is in constant danger from our own and other people's slanting.

One final aspect of slanted language which we should consider is the deliberate use of words which evoke strong, emotional responses from people. The author's purpose in doing this is not so much to create an impression which will influence his listeners or readers, but rather to excite them to the point where they will stop thinking and only experience emotion. The language used is meant to arouse anger, pity, prejudice, moral outrage, hate—whatever strong feelings will serve his purpose. He may praise one group excessively to win their sympathy, or may describe another group with derogatory language or words of ridicule to turn you against them.

Propagandists and politicians involved in smear campaigns often resort to this use of emotionally charged slanting. We may call it loaded language because of the weight of emotional connotations which the words carry.

The passage below contains some advice to lawyers on how to win cases against railroad companies when suing them on behalf of injured employees. It helps to make clear the use and purpose of loaded language. Look for words and phrases which you think might arouse certain emotions among the jurors who would have to decide a case.

Suing a railroad is not like suing "the little old lady on her way to church driving her Chevrolet," Robert N. Stone, chairman of the association's Railroad Law Section advised about 60 other lawyers who specialize in suing railroads on behalf of injured employees.

"Your goal," he said, "is to dehumanize the defendant."

This means driving it into the jurors' heads that this "conglomerate" owns coal mines and land development companies and big railroads and small railroads and is "a nonliving entity without the blood flowing through its veins and without the passion in its heart and without the concern for human beings."

He spat out a series of loaded questions he said he asks potential jurors in jury selection.

The purpose is to make sure that by the time the jury has been chosen, every member "knows that you're not dealing with just a little rinky-dink railroad that runs from Minneapolis to Chicago that may be going broke," but with "a huge corporate complexity that owns half the country."

To get in the mood for such a rhetorical tour de force, Mr. Stone counseled trial lawyers should reread Mark Antony's speech in *Julius Caesar*, which begins with an appeal to "Friends, Romans, countrymen."

The title of Mr. Stone's speech: "The Use of Language and Loaded Words in Cases Against Railroads and Other Large Corporations."

Exercise IV—Labels

Look at the words and phrases below. They are used as labels to identify an individual, a class of people, or a group in a particular way. The people who use them want to pin labels on their opponents or their own champions. Underline once the words or phrases which are intended to suggest something favorable or desirable, and underline twice words or phrases which are intended to attach an unfavorable or derogatory label.

PLAIN FOLKS LOUDMOUTH BIG BUSINESS SHIFTY-EYED

BLEEDING HEART RED SYMPATHIZER IVORY TOWER GODLESS

FANATIC FLATHEAD LOW CLASS INNOCENT VICTIM MACHO

DERANGED CITIFIED SOCIALIZED TRIGGER HAPPY HATE MONGERING

MAN OF THE PEOPLE   STAR-STUDDED   MOST AMAZING   JERKWATER TOWN
SKYROCKETING   SMALL-TIME   IGNORAMUS   IMPERIALIST
TRAMPLING ON THE RIGHTS   THE GREATEST   DECENT PEOPLE
RIGHT-THINKING   NASTY-MINDED   FREEDOM LOVING   FASCIST

Next, choose five labels from the group above and write a sentence for each which will put a person or a group in a favorable or sympathetic light. Circle the labels you used in the sentence.

1. ______________________________

2. ______________________________

3. ______________________________

4. ______________________________

5. ______________________________

Now choose five words or phrases from the list above and write a sentence which will put a person or a group in a negative, undesirable light. Circle the labels which you used in the sentence.

1. ______________________________

2. ______________________________

3. ______________________________

4. ______________________________

5. ______________________________

Our job, as listeners and readers who are trying to keep our thinking clear and deal with facts and issues logically, is to defuse the emotionally charged words. By recognizing slanted language for what it is we can get back on the road to thinking about the issue. Showing strong emotion doesn't necessarily mean that the person doing so is wrong, only that he may be clouding or confusing the issue. We want to understand an author's meaning and grasp the conclusions we were meant to reach. Strong feelings about an issue belong to the author; the decision to agree or disagree belongs to us.

B. Figurative Language

One of the best ways to add variety to our language in order to make it more interesting and more colorful is the use of figures of speech—in particular, similes, metaphors, and analogies. They are useful and effective because they give us images (pictures), thus bringing our senses into play and dressing up difficult or complicated ideas in clothes which we can recognize and admire. For instance, it is more interesting to say, "He's as strong as a bull" or "Her hair is like silk," than "He's very strong" or "She has nice hair." These figures of speech make comparisons for us so that we can say in a few words what it would take a long explanation to accomplish, and they do it in a far more exciting way.

A simile merely compares one thing with another, using *like* or *as* to bring the two things together.

A metaphor makes a comparison but it does not use the words *like* or *as*. *They behave like animals* is a simile. *Those people are vultures* is a metaphor.

An analogy is a more complicated comparison, involving a relationship between or among things. We use analogies to illustrate the way things function or to make a process easier to understand, as in the following:

> Running for political office is the same as walking a tightrope. One false move and you're out. Make it to the other side and you're a hero.

This analogy illustrates the relationship between the dangers and the rewards of both activities to point up the situation of a candidate for political office. In some standardized tests you may be asked to complete a series of word relationships similar to the analogy above. For example, the test question may read:

> Choose one of the four words listed which will complete the relationship between the first three terms.
>
> Man: boy :: woman: ___________
>
> 1. family 2. age 3. child 4. girl.

That is to say, man is to boy as woman is to ___________? The answer is 4. girl. Why? Because the relationship between the terms *man* and *boy* and *woman* and *girl* is the same; *boy* and *girl* designate the younger version of the adult male and female.

Similes, metaphors, and analogies are very helpful to our understanding, but we have to remember that they are only figures of speech; not evidence or proof. One thing may be like another in many ways, but it is not the same thing. People who want to persuade would like us to think that they are the same. An advertisement on television says that a particular brand of aspirin is "like a doctor's prescription." It is not a doctor's prescription and you would be deceived if you assumed that it would be equally effective. A comparison illuminates ideas and gives us a lead into understanding new and difficult concepts. When it serves that purpose only it is helpful and legitimate to use. It creates a problem for clear thinking when it is used as a basis for an argument. People jump to conclusions when they accept the similarities as facts.

To refute an argument based on a simile or a metaphor is fairly easy to do. You simply point out that the things being compared are not exactly the same, whatever their similarities may be. In the example given above which suggested that the advertised product would help you the same way as a doctor's prescription, you could point out that a prescription is given to help cure a particular illness; the ingredients are selected for a person with that particular illness or pain. The patent medicine is not a specific remedy. Similes and metaphors can never be literally true; in the previous examples given people are not wild animals, people are not vultures, men are not bulls, nor is hair silk.

To refute an argument based on an analogy the best approach is to attack the similarities which are assumed to exist. For example, in the analogy given above which compares the act of walking a tightrope and running for political office, it is assumed that the dangers are the same. However, the danger of falling from a high wire and the danger of losing an election are not the same. Losing may be a disappointment, but it is not an accident which could cause serious injury or death.

Another way to refute an argument which uses the relationship between things to prove a point is to extend the analogy, adding new similarities which will make the comparison meaningless. For instance, getting back to the tightrope walker and the political candidate, the tightrope walker has spectators to watch him succeed or fail, but the candidate has voters and they decide whether he will win or lose. Thus the comparison breaks down and an argument is defeated in an analogy when it is extended because no relationships can ever be identical in all ways.

Exercise V—Using Figurative Language

In the ten sentences which follow, some of the figures of speech illuminate an idea and stop there. They do not try to persuade us to reach a conclusion from the comparisons made. Others, however, go beyond helpful comparisons to argue a case.

First, identify the figure of speech used in the sentence by writing either *simile, metaphor,* or *analogy* on the line below it.

Second, if the writer is making an argument from the figure of speech, write the word *argument.*

Third, find the flaw in the argument by pointing out where the similarities assumed in the comparison fail to be real similarities, or where the comparison has been extended to the point it breaks down.

EXAMPLES

A. The prosecuting attorney's voice was a machine gun firing questions at the witness.

Metaphor

B. My history teacher says that getting grades in school is to education what harvesting is to farming; as you sow, you are like to reap.

Analogy Argument

The farmer plants and harvests his crops; the student studies and gets his grades. The farmer needs soil, sun, and water; the student needs intelligence, work, and materials. But the similarities end there because nature does the growing for the farmer; the effort of the student does the growing for him. Furthermore, nature is impersonal and indifferent to the farmer; the teacher's grade may not always be so.

1. Justice is a blindfolded goddess holding scales. Crime makes one side of the scale drop; punishment brings it back into balance.

2. Social Security is nothing more than a system of robbing Peter to pay Paul. The only question is: Whom will they rob to pay Peter?

3. Water seeks its own level and so do prices in our economy. If you interfere with the natural flow you are going to mess up the supply of drinking water. If you enforce price controls, you are going to interfere with the natural law of supply and demand.

4. All the world's a stage,
And all the men and women merely players.

Shakespeare, *As You Like It*

5. His speech was like a phonograph that played only one record. You knew exactly what he was going to say and how he was going to say it; you'd heard it all before.

6. Don't blame the television producers if you think that most of the programs are tasteless and boring. Television shows are manufactured to be sold like automobiles or any other product. So producers, like car manufacturers, should be free to make any kind of programs which they think will sell.

7. Authority is a gift which people give to their leaders. Like many gifts it is given because people feel that it has been earned, and so, like any gift, you should not ask that the receiver give it back.

8. His need to win was a fire that never died.

9. If you make it illegal for people to own handguns you are doing the same thing as if you prevented them

from installing a burglar alarm system in their homes. A man's home is his castle and he has the right to protect himself against criminals who break into his home.

____

____

____

10. We have to balance the national budget the same way a family has to balance its budget. If we go into debt by spending more than we earn then we'll go broke. The family has to keep within its income; so must our country.

____

____

____

C. Empty Language

If you have ever tried to answer an essay question when you didn't have the facts or the answers in your head then you know what padding is. You say the same thing two or three times in as many different ways. You use as many words as you can to fill up the space. Speakers and writers sometimes do the same thing. What they are saying may sound very good; their vocabulary may be excellent, but it's difficult to figure out what they have said. It's possible to read several paragraphs in a book and realize that the author has yet to make a point or tell us something we didn't already know. Let's call this verbiage—many important or pleasant sounding words with very little meaning. Politicians, diplomats, and business executives are often good at this kind of language because they must appear to be answering a question even though they don't know the answer or they do not want to give out the information they have been asked for. In everyday discussions people often talk at length, saying nothing, because they don't wish to appear uninformed or stupid. Just as with the formal speaker or the writer, it might have been better if they had declined to respond or chosen not to write about the subject. You can't get away with language which is empty of thought for very long.

We are more patient with each other in talking than we are in reading. If someone uses tired, worn-out words or expressions, we go along with them because speech is fast and we can move on to more interesting things quickly. But when we take the time to read or to study we want full value for our time and effort. If we don't get it we lose interest and stop reading, or skip over it quickly. Sometimes the author is at fault. Instead of making the effort to find interesting ways to present his material, he has taken the easy way out by using clichés. Unfortunately, many of those words and expressions have been so overworked that they are meaningless. This is called triteness. Like verbiage, which is used more to impress than to enlighten, triteness hinders communication with words which have no substance. Both forms require that we translate the empty language into our own words to get the meaning. With verbiage we eliminate unnecessary words and state the message clearly.

For example:

I would very much like to say that my purpose in addressing you today on the subject of our present and on-going practices to reduce state expenditures towards balancing the budget is primarily to enlist your support in these important endeavors.

becomes

I'm here because I want you to support my budget.

When we encounter triteness we are often dealing not only with worn-out expressions, but, more importantly, with worn-out ideas. We want to know what the person with whom we are communicating thinks and feels, but we can't do that if his language is full of clichés like *It stands to reason, built-in safeguards, the exception that proves the rule, on unimpeachable authority, from time immemorial, other things being equal,* and any other of the hundreds of expressions which have lost their impact and their meaning because they have been used too much and often without original thought.

For example, in the following passage, would you know how the speaker felt about his day in the country beyond the enthusiasm he shows?

> It was the greatest. I mean we really had a ball. We got up at the crack of dawn and made good time zooming up the highway. In no time, we left behind the hustle and bustle of the city streets and found ourselves in God's country, filling our lungs with fresh, country air and taking in the terrific views.

A simple translation might be, "We left the crowded city early in the morning and drove fast, enjoying the fresh air and scenery of the countryside." That is what is being said, but what personal account are we getting in the communication? Is there any way to respond other than, "That's nice"?

We have discussed verbiage and triteness together because they both hinder communication by using words carelessly—either more words than are necessary or words that are almost useless to convey meaning. We are impatient with speakers or authors who are verbose or trite, but we are not seriously blocked from getting their meaning. Jargon, however, the next kind of empty language we will examine, is more than a hindrance to communication—it is an enemy of clear thinking and a block to accurate communication.

Jargon is vocabulary peculiar to a profession, art, science, or class. Education, sociology, law, the military, government, and commerce all have their own vocabularies. The people who know and use the special words of their professions have no problems with their technical language. But when they use it to explain something to the general public they often appear to be speaking gibberish. For instance, the following statement is one which a sociologist might make to explain the behavior of a group—if he resorted to jargon. What do you think it means?

> The economically underprivileged and educationally deprived segment of any society can be seen under stressful circumstances to actuate their repressed hostilities in aggressive behavior patterns against that segment whose life-style gives evidence of affluence and access to political manipulation.

If, on the other hand, he wanted to speak plain English and say the same thing, he would have said, "In difficult times the poor and uneducated fight against the rich and powerful." Some examples of jargon are:

Education—*learning resource center* for *library*
language arts for *English*
classroom situation for *classroom*

Science *(especially the new sciences, psychology and sociology)*
conversational interaction for *talk*

Military—*airborne neutralization program* for *bombing*

Government—*informational input* for *memo*

We encounter jargon every day on radio, television, in newspapers, magazines, textbooks, speeches, and lectures. Corporate executives, military leaders, politicians, government officials, and academic authorities in different fields will use jargon at times to evade stating the simple truth. They may want to impress an audience with pretentious words and technical terms, or to make unpopular ideas less objectionable. "Excessing" people in a company sounds less ruthless than firing them. Saying that enemy troops were "liquidated" will have less of an impact on the public than saying that enemy troops were killed.

Many technical terms in the sciences cannot be put into simpler words because they represent a concept which is specific and peculiar to one field of study. We can accept such terms and learn their meanings. What we should be able to expect from specialists and authorities in various fields is that they use straightforward words and expressions when they communicate, not abstract, obscure, and highly technical language that comes across to the public as double-talk. The prospects for clear communication given in simple language which the non-professional person can understand will never be good as long as there are specialists who want to disguise the truth or who do not make the effort to be understood. We will always have to struggle to translate jargon to reach meaning.

Exercise VI—Words, Words, Words

In each of the selections below there are examples of verbiage, triteness, or some form of jargon. Identify each of these hindrances to clear communication by writing either *verbose, trite,* or *jargon* below each passage. Then rewrite the selection in straightforward English to make the meaning as clear, concise, or free from overused expressions as possible.

1. As listeners, our senses function as input reception centers which register external stimuli on our consciousness. However, not all stimuli registered is consistent with the intended input stimuli of the transmitter.

____

____

____

____

2. Even if you are of the opinion that some of the women's libbers have gone overboard in their demands, you have to bear in mind that, nowadays, the "little woman" is no longer just a homemaker. More and more, she's out there in the business world bringing home the bacon just like her spouse. So if the weaker sex wants to work right alongside the truck-drivers, the engineers, the State Troopers, or, for that matter, in any of the macho occupations, she should have a fair shake. A lot of right-minded people think this is an idea whose time has come.

____

____

____

____

3. When I asked the specialist how good my chances of full recovery were, he told me that the tests indicated a negative prognosis. He said there was no evidence of remission in the causative factors of my disorder. He's going to try a different antibiotic.

____

____

____

____

4. Insofar as this is the last occasion on which we shall meet as a group, I would like to take this opportunity to thank each and every one of you for the interest and cooperation which you have demonstrated at

all times for endeavors we have undertaken mutually. It has been and will continue to be a source of satisfaction to me personally to have been part of this organization.

____

____

____

____

5. Given the myriad complexities of the problem, which may strike us as being impervious to a facile resolution, it is encouraging, nonetheless, to reflect on past circumstances in which difficulties of equal proportion have confronted us and were found to be susceptible to relatively simple solutions.

____

____

____

____

6. Implementing new regulations from the Bureau of the Budget will effectuate additional fiscal burdens. As a consequence, corporate planning envisions a freeze on personnel acquisition.

____

____

____

____

3

Expressing Thoughts

A. Kinds of Sentences

We communicate our ideas and our beliefs when we make statements about them in the form of declarative sentences. A statement presents a fact or an opinion. It can be a report, a judgment, a proposition, or a comment. Whatever the form our assertion may take we are declaring what we think about an issue; we are saying that something is either true or false. Other people may agree or disagree with our statements. They may challenge our facts or question the soundness of our opinions. We enter into the area of argument when we exchange statements.

We can express thoughts in forms other than statements. For instance, we can ask questions, show emotion, make requests or give commands using other types of sentences. But only statements (declarative sentences) can be true or false. Arguing for or against an issue means making statements about it and arriving at a conclusion.

In this chapter we will be concerned with arguments—the attempts people make to persuade us to their way of thinking and convince us that their opinions are sound. We are expected to form opinions and draw conclusions in every aspect of our lives. How well we do this will depend on our ability to separate facts from opinions, good arguments from poor ones.

A discussion is a collection of sentences put together by the people participating in the discussion. The sentences are made up of statements, questions, expressions of emotion, reasons, and conclusions. If the speaker or writer has been careful, the sentences will be arranged to make his opinions as convincing as possible. In advertising, profits are at stake and great care is taken to design a presentation that will persuade you to buy a particular product. Political careers depend upon the candidates' ability to get votes, or convince others to support their causes. A great deal of the nonfiction we read is an attempt to convince us to adopt new ideas or to change those we have. To keep our thinking clear so that we can reach sound conclusions, we have to evaluate statements. We must decide what is true, what is reasonable.

The first step is to identify statements; to recognize an assertion that is being made and separate it from everything else that is said. For example, read the following passage and decide which of the sentences make a statement:

What an election! The Republicans won every state but six. What do you think about that? The number of people who voted this year was bigger than in the last five years. So, the Democrats can't say that it was failure to vote that defeated them: There's a new movement in the country. People want to return to more conservative policies. Join the conservatives and be with the winners.

What an election! is an exclamatory sentence which shows surprise and delight.

The Republicans won every state but six is a statement. It states a fact.

What do you think about that? is a question. It may or may not require an answer.

The number of people who voted this year was bigger than in the last five years is another statement of fact.

So, the Democrats can't say that it was failure to vote that defeated them is a statement in the form of an opinion.

There's a new movement in the country is a statement of opinion also.

People want to return to more conservative policies is another statement of opinion.

Join the conservatives and be with the winners is an imperative sentence. It commands with the imperative words *join* and *be with*.

The speaker mixed a variety of sentence forms presenting statements of fact and opinion with a show of some emotion and a strong suggestion for you to do something. He has presented an argument because he gave reasons to support a conclusion: people voted for the Republicans and against the Democrats because he thinks that there is a growing movement towards more conservative thinking. He wants you to support this movement.

Whether he has made a good or a poor argument for his belief depends upon how accurate his facts are and how well-founded his opinions. We can prove his statements about the results of the election by checking the election records. If the Republicans won every state but six, and the number of people voting was bigger than it has been in the last five years, then those statements are true; he has stated facts. If you think that these facts are sufficient to justify his opinions about why the Democrats lost, and that there is a new movement in the country, you may be convinced that he is right. On the other hand, if you can think of any reasons—statements of fact and opinion—to refute his claim of a new movement or other causes of the Democratic defeat, you will disagree and choose not to "be with the winners."

The clue to determining that the passage was an argument is in the word *so*. The statements which preceded it explain a situation. Many things we read and hear are only exposition; they clarify a situation or an issue. When we encounter words like *so, therefore,* and *consequently,* we recognize that the author is moving from exposition into argument. He is going to use his statements as reasons to justify a conclusion. He expects us to draw inferences from his statements—that is, to reason with him to reach a conclusion.

Exercise I—Statements

In the sentences below draw a circle around the number before each sentence which makes a statement (a report, a judgment, a proposition, or a comment which asserts something).

1. What a terrible thing to happen!
2. They made their flight connection with only minutes to spare.
3. Lock the doors and close the windows before the storm comes.
4. Why do you suppose I asked you to bring them along?
5. Good Grief! Charlie Brown.
6. If the number of graduate students in engineering continues to increase at the present rate, there will be no managerial jobs available to them in ten years.
7. Don't ask me that again.
8. They followed the blueprints for the construction of the new library.
9. Even if I had studied harder I still couldn't have passed that test.
10. Am I right or wrong?
11. When people make statements which they offer as reasons they usually say "because", "since", or "in view of the fact".
12. The right of free speech is limited by laws about obscene language and libel.
13. We refused to pay the total bill of the contractors because they doubled the estimated cost.

14. Didn't I tell you? They've already left.

15. People who change their opinions have undisciplined minds. Right?

B. Facts or Opinions?

We have seen that any discussion which is leading to a conclusion contains statements of fact and opinion. The facts must be pertinent to the issue and they must offer good reasons to form the opinions in order to persuade us. People often present us with impressive facts which have no bearing on the argument. We say, "That's true, but what has it got to do with this case?" We sometimes challenge a conclusion because the facts do not reasonably justify the conclusion.

In spoken arguments people do not always take the trouble to present their statements in an orderly, logical way. They go back and forth between facts and opinions, strong expressions of feeling, and comments about what we should think or do. To keep your thinking clear you have to select the factual information and limit your responses to what is accurate and reasonable. The task is easier when you are reading newspaper editorials, magazine articles, or other forms of argument in print, because the personal and emotional impact of the speaker is missing. You have more time to judge and consider. There is no guarantee, however, that because the argument appears in print it will be sound and logical.

We must be able to differentiate between what is a fact and what is an opinion. They are often connected in confusing ways. A fact is a true statement. It is true because it can be verified by observation, by experience, or by consulting sources which have confirmed its accuracy. It is an event or something that has actual existence.

An opinion is a belief, a view, or a judgment about someone or something. It is more than an impression, but it is not positive knowledge. If someone says, "I have the feeling that this would not be a good thing for us to do," he is expressing a vague, indefinite belief. If he says, "I do not think that this would be a good thing for us to do," he is stating an opinion. He may or may not be correct in his judgment, but he must be prepared to defend it, since we hold people accountable for their opinions.

Exercise II—Separating Fact from Opinion

In the sentences below write either *fact* or *opinion* on the line below each sentence.

1. Just because a few people cheated doesn't mean that the whole class is dishonest.

   ____

2. Eating raw fish will make you sick.

   ____

3. If all the promises and threats which politicians make at election time came true, we would be swamped with benefits we couldn't afford and dangers we couldn't survive.

   ____

4. Jack is taller than Bob, but not as tall as Fred.

   ____

5. The union rank and file refused to ratify the contract.

   ____

6. I warned him not to go swimming after eating a big meal, but he thinks that's just a foolish notion.

7. Our laboratory tests reveal that EASYTUM tablets are the most effective antacid preparation you can take.

8. In his first year in office he did more to help this country than any other president did in full four years of office.

9. They were foolish to challenge his facts in the case.

10. Mark Twain said, "The difference between the right word and the almost right word is the difference between lightning and the lightning bug."

11. It's the best selling home computer on the market.

12. It's the most entertaining video game available.

13. We should encourage them in their efforts to improve the environment.

14. The jury deliberated for twelve hours before deciding on a verdict of guilty for the defendant.

15. If you think it over I'm sure that you will agree with us that we have no other choice but to ask for his resignation.

C. Conclusions—Valid or Invalid?

We have used the word *argument* in this chapter to mean any spoken or written discourse which attempts to persuade. Arguments are not limited to formal debates or, in the popular use of the word, to disagreements. When a group of sentences contains at least two statements of fact and opinion, one of the statements will be a reason and the other will be a conclusion, the reason supporting the conclusion. For example, sentence number nine in the previous exercise states, "They were foolish to challenge his facts in the case." It is an opinion. It would have been a statement of fact if it had read, "They challenged his facts in the case." Neither would be an argument. But if it had read, "They were foolish to challenge his facts in the case because he had thoroughly checked every statement he made" it would be an argument. The conclusion "They were foolish to challenge his facts" is supported by the reason "he had thoroughly checked every statement he made."

We can distinguish facts from opinions easily if we listen and read carefully and critically. We can separate the conclusions we are meant to draw from the reasons given to justify them by analyzing the author's reasoning and by looking for clues such as the words *because, since,* and *for* before reasons, and *so, consequently,* and *therefore* before conclusions. If the reasons are not based on pertinent facts or if the conclusion does not follow logically from the reasons, then the author is to blame. If we don't recognize the inconsistency in the author's thinking, then we can be faulted for believing what may not be true.

A conclusion is a reasoned judgment. It is a valid conclusion if the facts offered as reasons support it; it is invalid if they fail to support it or do not lead you reasonably to the same judgment. Whether a conclusion is clearly stated or only implied, the test of its being valid or invalid, that is, sound or unsound, lies in the exercise of your own good sense. You must ask yourself if the statements made are accurate and relevant and whether you can draw the same inference from them which the author does.

In conversation or in class discussions you will often hear people say, "But that's not my point," or "No, I didn't mean that," or "But, I didn't say that." They often argue about the conclusion before they have grasped the point being made. They confuse conclusions with reasons and facts with opinions. In reading arguments such as those we encounter in textbooks, it is possible to go back and reread the statements to be sure that we have understood them. But in discussions, we are reluctant to ask the speaker to repeat parts of the argument. Often, there doesn't seem to be time to pause and consider the statements. Nonetheless, whether we are listening to or reading a series of facts, opinions, reasons, and conclusions, it is crucial that we run the thoughts expressed through our minds before we decide to agree with or reject the conclusions presented. Fortunately, we can think in thousands of words a minute; we can listen to and read only hundreds of words a minute. There is time to hold many thoughts in our minds at the same time. If we stay with the reasoning the speaker or the author is sending us, we can arrive at our own reasoned judgments about his conclusions. It's a habit of thought as vital to learning as concentration is to developing physical skills.

Exercise III—Analyzing Arguments

For each of the twenty selections which appear below:

I. Underline once the statements which are facts and underline twice the statements which are opinions.
II. If the selection contains a conclusion (stated or implied), write the conclusion on the first line below the selection and the reason or reasons given to support it on the following lines.
III. Finally, write *valid* if you think the conclusion is justified by the facts given, *invalid* if you are not convinced by the author's facts or reasoning.

1. The people demonstrating in front of City Hall are from out of town. They have no jobs and no money. They don't want to work and they came here just to stir up trouble.

____

____

____

____

2. Another series of malfunctions and broken-down equipment caused a three-hour delay on the commuter train this morning. When is the railroad company going to do something about this dangerous situation? They charge enough for the fare to run a decent and safe railway system.

____

____

____

____

3. He was the last one to leave the locker room. I know because the coach said he locked up as soon as he left. Also, he was the only one who knew my combination. I gave it to him to get my books when I was out sick last week. I hate to accuse a friend, but he must have taken my radio.

4. I ate in the cafeteria for the first time in a month. I was sick all night.

5. Public opinion polls aren't worth very much. Politicians are always surprised after an election. What people tell a reporter about how they are going to vote and how they actually vote can be very different. Also, people change their minds at the last minute for a lot of reasons.

6. More people are staying home now because the price of tickets to the movies or the theater or to big concerts is climbing higher and higher. A lot of people have cable TV now and more people are buying video machines and cassettes. They figure, "Why go out and waste money?"

7. You should never criticize anybody. We're all human and we all make mistakes.

8. She's lovely. She's a star. She uses KREME-MOR soap.

9. It's time to admit defeat and close down the plant. Sales are off by forty percent. We can't meet next month's payroll and the bank refuses to give us another loan.

10 I waited an hour and ten minutes for her. She never called. I guess I'm just not her type.

11 Whenever the Democrats are in power there's a war. When the Republicans are in power there's a depression. What we need is a third party.

12. Hitler started World War II.

13. That was a really bad movie. Nothing happened in two hours and the acting was terrible.

14. It's best to take a middle-of-the-road course in politics. That way you'll never become too conservative or too liberal. It's safer for the country as a whole.

15. The committee met last week, gathered all the papers pertinent to the case, and interviewed all the participants. They will release their findings later this month.

16. In view of the fact that some foods are better for you than others, we must conclude that some foods are not good for you.

17. The First Amendment guarantees free speech, so anyone should be able to say anything he wants to.

18. You can see that it is pointless to argue with her; she never listens to anyone else's ideas.

19. Men build houses, but women make homes.

20. Constitutional guarantees and present laws permit the private ownership of firearms. Because of a sharp increase in crime in recent times, many individuals have obtained guns and permits to own them. These individuals are exercising their rights under the law to possess firearms.

4

Organizing Thoughts

A. Patterns of Organization

Students have an added responsibility for communication in school which they don't have anywhere else. They must not only follow arguments which they encounter in lectures and in textbook reading, but they must also be able to reconstruct them. To be successful, students must be able to demonstrate that they have understood the conclusions drawn and the reasons presented to justify an argument. Because students are dealing with newly acquired information and unfamiliar concepts in many different fields of study, teachers require them to prove that they can reason as the author did to reach his conclusions. Through questions in class discussion and tests, through essays which ask the student to explain the author's argument as it was presented, students are obliged to reconstruct what they have learned.

In everyday encounters with persuasive material we are not asked to repeat in elaborate detail the course of an argument. We think about it and either agree or disagree. Learning requires an added step before we respond with our own reasoned judgment. Lengthy discussions in class, whole chapters of a textbook, pages of additional required reading, all demand that students retain a tremendous amount of information. If you, as a student, are going to be able to reconstruct all this material, you will first have to see how it was organized. If you understand the organizational structure, you will better be able to remember the material in an orderly sequence.

Details (pieces of information) are difficult to remember; ideas and concepts stay in our memories longer. For example, you may not be able to remember and repeat every detail given in a chapter which explained the events leading to World War II, but you are likely to retain the concepts of ruthless aggression, religious persecution, and Hitler's plan to dominate Europe. We can recall important details when we see how they are related to major ideas. To remember accurately, we have to proceed *from* ideas *to* factual details.

If you were writing a letter to a friend, you would record your thoughts as they came to you. But, if you were writing an essay for an examination, you would first plan how you intend to present the ideas you learned from your reading. Any long argument or explanation requires an organized plan; a logical sequence of reasons and conclusions.

In this chapter we will examine six patterns or methods of organization which are commonly used to present material in an orderly sequence. Recognizing these patterns in your reading will help you to understand and remember textbook material so that you can reconstruct it accurately. In a lecture or a large section of a textbook, an author may use several or all of the patterns, but each one is a key to remembering major ideas.

The patterns of organization are:

1. Time Order
2. Comparison and Contrast
3. Cause and Effect
4. Enumeration
5. Extended Definition
6. Analogy

1. TIME ORDER — A sequence of events as they happened. Dates may be used, or clues like *first, next, before that, after that.*

The tradition of tool- and diemaking is as old as the industrial age. Many of the earliest practitioners were blacksmiths who turned their forging talents to toolmaking. In the 18th century, craftsmen gathered in the manufacturing hubs of England, France, Germany and Sweden to fashion tools that would enable machines to produce items like clocks and locks. The trade flourished most dramatically in America. In the early 1800s, Eli Whitney helped to pioneer mass production, using standardized, interchangeable parts of his Connecticut musket factory. By the early 1900s, the toolmaker's skills enabled machines to engrave the Lord's Prayer on a sliver of metal less than one-hundredth of an inch wide.

"In the 18th century," "In the early 1800s," and "by the early 1900s" set the time pattern.

2. COMPARISON AND CONTRAST — Similarities and differences are shown. Clue words are *just as, likewise, similarly, unlike, opposite.*

Just as the stonecutters who chiseled ornate facades for Europe's grand Gothic cathedrals were master craftsmen of the Middle Ages, tool- and diemakers are premier artisans of the industrial era. Instead of granite or limestone, their medium is hard metal. They create the tools that can cut metal into precise patterns and the dies to mold it into complex shapes.

"Just as" is the beginning of the comparison. "Instead of" indicates a major difference, a contrast.

3. CAUSE AND EFFECT — A condition exists; the cause, or reason, is given. Clue words are *resulted in, brought about, stemmed from.*

Unlike most nationality groups in the world today, the people of the United States are not ethnically rooted in the land where they live. The French have remote Gallic antecedents; the Germans, Teutonic; the English, Anglo-Saxon; the Italians, Roman; the Irish, Celtic; but the only people in America who can claim ancient American origins are a remnant of Red Indians. In any deep dimension of time, all other Americans are immigrants. They began as Europeans (or in the case of 10 per cent of the population, as Africans), and if they became Americans it was only, somehow, after a relatively recent passage westbound across the Atlantic.

The effect: All but a few Americans have no roots here. The cause: They "became" Americans. Contrast is used to state the effect.

4. ENUMERATION — A listing of reasons, facts, results, causes, aims, or questions is given.

The aims of punishment are:

1. Retribution
2. General deterrence
3. Special deterrence
4. Incapacitation
5. Reformation

The author may not number the items in a series, but may use *many factors, several reasons* or *among the causes* as clues to a list.

5. EXTENDED DEFINITION — Clarifies a meaning or explains a process. It is exposition, not argument.

Punishment is the unpleasant consequence which the penal law prescribes for socially undesired human conduct, and which criminal courts impose according to the laws of penal procedure. Or, briefly, punishment is the deliberate infliction of suffering.

6. ANALOGY — A comparison of the ways in which two different things relate. In this example, modern man and caged animals share a relationship.

In many respects, modern man is like a wild animal spending its life in a zoo; like the animal, he is fed abundantly and protected from inclemencies but deprived of the natural stimuli essential for many functions of his body and his mind. Man is alienated not only from other men, not only from nature, but more importantly from the deepest layers of his fundamental self.

Exercise I—Identifying Patterns

Read the paragraphs below and identify the pattern of organization which the author uses to present his material. Write the name of the pattern on the blank below each selection.

1. In all countries of Western civilization, the largest part of life is now spent in an environment conditioned and often entirely created by technology. Thus one of the most significant and disturbing aspects of modern life is that man's contacts with the rest of creation are almost always distorted by artificial means, even though his senses and fundamental perceptions have remained the same since the Stone Age. Modern man is anxious, even during peace and in the midst of economic affluence, because the technological world that constitutes his immediate environment, by separating him from the natural world under which he evolved, fails to satisfy certain of his unchangeable needs.

____

2. Today's artisans can trim metal to within one ten-thousandth of an inch, using mechanical cuts more precise than the strokes of the finest brain surgeon. During a grueling four-year apprenticeship in vocational classrooms and on the shop floor, the toolmaker absorbs the principles of solid geometry and learns to think in three dimensions. He is expected to read labyrinthine blueprints a well as be aware of the exact levels of heat and pressure that will cause various metals to buckle and break.

____

3. In the criminological literature, it is sometimes reported that in certain countries conditions of life within prisons have so improved that they are better than the conditions which some of the inmates are used to outside. If so, it is not impossible that there are poor people who commit crimes to achieve a better life in prison.

____

4. In the quest for other means to battle crime with the limited resources available, state officials are exploring other alternatives. One is to remove a number of less pressing offenses—spitting on the subways, for example, or garbage-can violations—from the jurisdiction of the Criminal Courts, clearing their dockets for more important matters. Another would provide mandatory community service as a punishment for lesser crimes—a system that has had some success in other jurisdictions.

____

5. Japanese management emphasizes teamwork and group performance. It rewards those who help make the team work better rather than individual stars. Unlike American management, which adheres to a church-state-like separation of work life and the life of "human values," Japanese management unabashedly links them through endless articulation of what the institution honors, values and believes. (Such values can range from Matsushita's "seven spiritual values" to Delta Airlines' emphasis on "service" to customers.)

____

6. The first of these is *the law of adaptation*. In every area that can support life, communities of plants and animals develop which are best adapted to this particular environment. They live here, not necessarily because they are the only ones that could survive here, but because they are able to excel all competitors in the struggle for available food and shelter.

---

7. Through the city of Los Angeles runs a canal lined with concrete. During some parts of the year this canal carries a thin trickle of water, the last vestige of what was once the Los Angeles River. Today the entire normal flow of this river runs through the pipes of the city water system to do its share in meeting the city's needs. Long ago the city outgrew this supply of water, but this was not too serious. There was a huge supply underground. Shallow wells produced enough for every additional need. As seemed right and proper, every man owned all the water beneath his land, and he was free to pump as much as he desired. The thriving city and its surrounding communities grew. Households and factories and irrigated farms all took their growing share of water. Slowly the level of the underground water began to sink. Wells were dug deeper, and still the water dropped. Like the river on the surface, this underground supply was fed by the flow from nearby mountains. It was so vast in extent that it gave the appearance of being inexhaustible. But when the demands outgrew the streams that fed it, this river too could go dry like the surface river, and it became apparent that the wells were drawing from the ground more than its entire income of water.

This passage and the two that follow each treat the subject of baseball differently to make their points. They use the same patterns effectively.

8. Deep down, I know baseball is just as crass and unruly as the real world, but I prefer the illusion: baseball as an amiable, ordered world contained within the neat geometry of a stadium. Colonel and cab driver alike can argue with fine equality about a player trade or a ninth-inning bunt. The rules are known to all, and the unending variations are available to all for interpretation.

---

9. The late Margaret Mead recognized baseball's role in a 1964 interview in which she said: "Baseball is to American boys what dressing and self-adornment are to American girls. Both are games, carried far beyond the necessities of life. Spending hours doing her hair, putting it in rollers and sitting under a mechanical dryer convince the teen-aged girl that she is indeed a girl. Spending endless hours playing baseball, talking about baseball, reading about baseball is one way for American boys to convince themselves that they are boys.

---

10. The game is quintessentially American in the way it puts the premium on both the individual and on the team; in the way it encourages enterprise and imagination and yet asserts the supreme power of the law. Baseball is quintessentially American in the way it tells us that much as you travel and far as you go, out to the green frontier, the purpose is to get home, back to where the others are. The pioneer is ever striving to come back to the common place. A nation of migrants always, for all the wandering, remembers what every immigrant never forgets: that you may leave home but if you forget where home is, you are truly lost and without hope.

Once we recognize the structure of a paragraph and see the pattern the author used to communicate his ideas and their supporting details, we are able to understand his thoughts and reconstruct them. In learning, it isn't enough to know what we have read; we have to be able to demonstrate that we have understood it. If we see structure, it is easier to reconstruct meaning when we are tested on the material.

Exercise II—Responding to Patterns

The ten passages from Exercise I are repeated below. Read each one again and answer the questions. As a further aid to helping you to recognize structure, the questions reveal the pattern used.

1. In all countries of Western civilization, the largest part of life is now spent in an environment conditioned and often entirely created by technology. Thus one of the most significant and disturbing aspects of modern life is that man's contacts with the rest of creation are almost always distorted by artificial means, even though his senses and fundamental perceptions have remained the same since the Stone Age. Modern man is anxious, even during peace and in the midst of economic affluence, because the technological world that constitutes his immediate environment, by separating him from the natural world under which he evolved, fails to satisfy certain of his unchangeable needs.

(a) What is the effect on modern man of living in a technological environment?

(b) What is the cause of his distress?

2. Today's artisans can trim metal to within one ten-thousandth of an inch using mechanical cuts more precise than the strokes of the finest brain surgeon. During a grueling four-year apprenticeship in vocational classrooms and on the shop floor, the toolmaker absorbs the principles of solid geometry and learns to think in three dimensions. He is expected to read labyrinthine blueprints as well as be aware of the exact levels of heat and pressure that will cause various metals to buckle and break.

(a) What is defined in this paragraph?

(b) List the details which define the requirements of the job.

3. In the criminological literature, it is sometimes reported that in certain countries conditions of life within prisons have so improved that they are better than the conditions which some of the inmates are used to outside. If so, it is not impossible that there are poor people who commit crimes to achieve a better life in prison.

(a) What effect has been observed by improving prison conditions in some countries?

(b) Why may this be so?

4. In the quest for other means to battle crime with the limited resources available, state officials are exploring other alternatives. One is to remove a number of less pressing offenses—spitting on the subways, for example, or garbage-can violations—from the jurisdiction of the Criminal Courts, clearing their dockets for more important matters. Another would provide mandatory community service as a punishment for lesser crimes—a system that has had some success in other jurisdictions.

From "The Crime-Without-Punishment Crisis," by Richard J. Meislin. ©1981 by the New York Times Company. Reprinted by permission.

(a) What is the problem facing state officials?

(b) List the alternatives they are considering and the possible benefits which they might bring about.

5. Japanese management emphasizes teamwork and group performance. It rewards those who help make the team work better rather than individual stars. Unlike American management, which adheres to a church-state-like separation of work life and the life of "human values," Japanese management unabashedly links them "through endless articulation of what the institution honors, values and believes. (Such values can range from Matsushita's "seven spiritual values" to Delta Airlines' emphasis on "service" to customers.)

From a book review by Urban Lehner. Reprinted by permission of *The Wall Street Journal,* ©Dow Jones & Company, Inc. 1981. All rights reserved.

In this comparison state the most significant differences between Japanese and American business practices.

6. The first of these is *the law of adaptation.* In every area that can support life, communities of plants and animals develop which are best adapted to this particular environment. They live here, not necessarily because they are the only ones that could survive here, but because they are able to excel all competitors in the struggle for available food and shelter.

From *The Web of Life* by John H. Storer. Copyright ©1981 by John H. Storer. Reprinted by permission of Devin-Adair Publishers.

(a) In this definition of a biological law, what part of the second sentence makes the important distinction?

(b) Write the 'law of adaptation.'

7. Through the city of Los Angeles runs a canal lined with concrete. During some parts of the year this canal carries a thin trickle of water, the last vestige of what was once the Los Angeles River. Today the entire normal flow of this river runs through the pipes of the city water system to do its share in meeting the city's needs. Long ago the city outgrew this supply of water, but this was not too serious. There was a huge supply underground. Shallow wells produced enough for every additional need. As seemed right and proper, every man owned all the water beneath his land, and he was free to pump as much as he desired. The thrivng city and its surrounding communities grew. Households and factories and irrigated farms all took their growing share of water. Slowly the level of the underground water began to sink. Wells were dug deeper, and still the water dropped. Like the river on the surface, this underground supply was fed by the flow from nearby mountains. It was so vast in extent that it gave the appearance of being inexhaustible. But when the demands outgrew the streams that fed it, this river too could go dry like the surface river, and it becme apparent that the wells were drawing from the ground more than its entire income of water.

In this sequence of events, list the order in which they occurred to reach the present condition.

8. Deep down, I know baseball is just as crass and unruly as the real world, but I prefer the illusion: baseball as an amiable, ordered world contained within the neat geometry of a stadium. Colonel and cab driver alike can argue with fine equality about a player trade or a ninth-inning bunt. The rules are known to all, and the unending variations are available to all for interpretation.

(a) What two unlike things are being compared?

(b) What relationships are cited between them which demonstrate the author's point?

9. The late Margaret Mead recognized baseball's role in a 1964 interview in which she said: "Baseball is to American boys what dressing and self-adornment are to American girls. Both are games, carried far beyond

the necessities of life. Spending hours doing her hair, putting it in rollers and sitting under a mechanical dryer convince the teen-aged girl that she is indeed a girl. Spending endless hours playing baseball, talking about baseball, reading about baseball is one way for American boys to convince themselves that they are boys."

(a) What is the function which baseball plays in our society according to the anthropologist, Margaret Mead?

(b) Write the analogy she makes.

(c) List the details which extend the analogy.

10. The game is quintessentially American in the way it puts the premium on both the individual and on the team; in the way it encourages enterprise and imagination and yet asserts the supreme power of the law. Baseball is quintessentially American in the way it tells us that much as you travel and far as you go, out to the green frontier, the purpose is to get home, back to where the others are. The pioneer is ever striving to come back to the common place. A nation of migrants always, for all the wandering, remembers what every immigrant never forgets: that you may leave home but if you forget where home is, you are truly lost and without hope.

(a) *Quintessentially* means "a most typical example." Write the three examples which the author enumerates.

(b) What is implied in the first sentence?

(c) What two very different objectives are compared here?

(d) Re-state the comparisons made in the last three sentences in the form of an analogy. First, identify the two different kinds of people mentioned and their similar activity.

B. Understanding and Remembering Accurately

Each chapter of this book has been concerned with aspects of communication vital to the primary needs of a student: to listen, to read, to understand, and to remember what is heard or read accurately. We explored individual words and the power they contain to suggest different meanings according to the way they are used. We saw that language can be used to make ideas clear and interesting, or it can be used to slant or prejudice thinking, or to cover up a lack of thinking.

In discussing the statements people make to declare their beliefs, we tried to distinguish between facts and opinions, and we searched for their conclusions about issues. We judged the soundness of their conclusions by the reasons they used in their attempt to convince us.

Finally, we examined some patterns which speakers and writers use to organize lengthy arguments designed to give us new ideas or to change those we may have. The selections chosen for the exercises in patterns of organization at the beginning of this chapter were typical of materials students must read in newspaper and magazine articles and textbooks. We emphasized the need for recognizing structure because students must be able to reproduce as well as understand the arguments presented in textbooks.

In the last exercise which follows you will have the opportunity to develop your skills in communicating the information and the ideas presented to you. The exercise will test your ability to *receive* the ideas accurately, that is, to read and understand fully. As the *sender,* that is, the student answering questions orally or in writing about what has been read, the test of your ability will be in how accurately you can reconstruct the materials you have read.

Exercise III—Understanding and Remembering Arguments

The ten selections used in this exercise are typical of the kind of required reading you might have to do for a class. The purpose of the exercise is to help you to understand the arguments given and, by arranging conclusions and supporting reasons logically, to reconstruct the arguments accurately.

First, read the selection to find the conclusion and write it on the lines provided.

Next, read the selection again to find the supporting reasons. Look for the pattern or patterns the author used to arrange them in order. Write the reasons on the lines provided.

EXAMPLE

After the year 1808 Napoleon's power and his ability to hold the vast European empire he had constructed began to weaken. Soon, it would collapse and the peoples he had forced into his vision of a united Europe would revolt and exile him to St. Helena. Why should so great a leader who held out the promise of political liberty and equality for the European nations fail in his attempt? For one thing, the empire was too large for any one man to manage and Napoleon was jealous of his power and reluctant to accept advice from others. Also, he had not unified the new Europe he had created in any lasting fashion. It was held together by military force and could dissolve as a result of military defeat. Lastly, and perhaps most significantly, his ruthless despotism encouraged a strong feeling of nationalism among the German and Italian rulers and among the common people who resented the presence of French officials and French officers and soldiers throughout their countries. Feelings of loyalty and nationalism seemed to have outweighed material and political interests.

CONCLUSION: Napoleon's vision of a united Europe failed to become a reality and he was removed from power. (That is the **effect,** the condition, which existed after 1808.)

REASONS: These are the **causes** which the author enumerates with the words *for one thing, also,* and *lastly.* 1. The empire was too large for one man to manage. 2. It was not really unified, only militarily forced together. 3. National loyalties were aroused by the presence of the French everywhere in German and Italian countries. 4. These people preferred loyalty to their country to the benefits which the empire promised.

1. **A Story of Mastery** • Civilization is, then, a story of mastery. To primitive man nature was an enemy. Driven by hunger, cold, and storms, he believed that the earth was filled with evil spirits who sought to harm him. Gradually he began to discover nature's secrets and understand her ways. Later he learned to direct her forces. Nature was then no longer his enemy, but his friend and helper. Slowly at first, but with ever-growing success, he spread his control over the world around him. As we follow his progress through the long years to the present time, we see how he conquered the problem of hunger and cold, how he overcame distance, how he pushed into the unknown and discovered all parts of the globe, how he trained his mind through education and conquered fear through knowledge, how he ruled his spirit through religion. Today we find that he has even learned how to extend his physical powers. With his telescope he can see thousands of miles through space, and with his microscope he can examine organisms previously invisible to the human eye. His ear can hear voices and sounds throughout the globe. He can wing his way through the heavens like a bird, and he can travel through the waters like a fish.

CONCLUSION: ______________________________

____

____

____

REASONS: ______________________________

____

____

____

____

____

2. In the course of history many more people have died for their drink and their dope than have died for their religion or their country. The craving for ethyl alcohol and the opiates has been stronger, in these millions, than the love of God, of home, of children; even of life. Their cry was not for liberty or death; it was for death preceded by enslavement. There is a paradox here, and a mystery. Why should such multitudes of men and women be so ready to sacrifice themselves for a cause so utterly hopeless and in ways so painful and so profoundly humiliating?

To this riddle there is, of course, no simple or single answer. Human beings are immensely complicated creatures, living simultaneously in a half dozen different worlds. Each individual is unique and, in a number of respects, unlike all the other members of the species. None of our motives is unmixed, none of our actions can be traced back to a single source and, in any group we care to study, behavior patterns that are observably similar may be the result of many constellations of dissimilar causes.

Thus, there are some alcoholics who seem to have been biochemically predestined to alcoholism. (Among rats, as Prof. Roger Williams, of the University of Texas, has shown, some are born drunkards; some are born teetotalers and will never touch the stuff.) Other alcoholics have been foredoomed not by some inherited defect in their biochemical make-up, but by their neurotic reactions to distressing events in their childhood or adolescence. Again, others embark upon their course of slow suicide as a result of mere imitation and good fellowship because they have made such an "excellent adjustment to their group"—a process which, if the group happens to be criminal, idiotic or merely ignorant, can bring only disaster to the well-adjusted individual. Nor must we forget that large class of addicts who have taken to drugs or drink in order to escape from physical pain. Aspirin, let us remember, is a very recent invention. Until late in the Victorian era, "poppy and mandragora," along with henbane and ethyl alcohol, were the only pain relievers available to civilized man. Toothache, arthritis and neuralgia could, and frequently did, drive men and women to become opium addicts.

CONCLUSION: ______________________________

____

REASONS:

3. That a just government should rest upon the consent of the governed assuredly is as true today as it was when the Declaration of Independence was signed. Equally true is the principle that the people, when properly consulted, remain the most trustworthy source of that underlying and continuing wisdom needed when great choices have to be made—above all, choices of those representatives capable of providing leadership in political matters. But to move from these truths to the position that is now becoming so widely accepted, that opinion—of the kind that can be instantly ascertained by any poll or survey—must somehow govern, must therefore be incessantly studied, courted, flattered, and drawn upon in lieu of the judgment which true leadership alone is qualified to make in the operating details of government—this is the great heresy, and also the "fatal malady" (as Walter Lippmann called it) of modern democracies.

CONCLUSION:

REASONS:

4. Though American technique is the envy of the world, the "American Way of Life" does not command unqualified respect abroad. We have proved to all the peoples of the earth that it is possible for an energetic nation to raise its material and civic standards to undreamed-of heights. The example has been zealously studied. Other nations are eager to adopt our magic formula. Yet they are reluctant to accept the idea that the American brand of technology provides the ultimate blueprint for the good life. Indeed, we ourselves are beginning to suspect that economic abundance and civic freedom may not be enough.

Wherein have we failed?

In this attempt to analyze some of our shortcomings and to suggest remedies, I draw from my experience as an educator and practicing architect both in this country and abroad. I have had considerable opportunity to observe the impact of American culture on older countries, especially those which have recently emerged from a feudal or colonial past into the pattern of a modern industrial society. Everywhere the introduction of mechanization has produced such confusion that the problems of the conversion have been more evident than the benefits.

I have become more and more convinced that we have failed to give leadership in the right direction. We have not exported, along with our technical and scientific skills, principles of wise application—mainly because we have not formulated such principles at home. For example, our biggest man-made objects—our cities—have steadily grown more chaotic and ugly, despite brilliant individual contributions to planning and design. For all the heroic efforts of conservationists, a good deal of our loveliest countryside is being bulldozed out of existence, a sacrifice to commerical exploitation. In our smaller towns people try hard to preserve a certain regional character and community spirit—a losing struggle against the conformity imposed by mass production. Increasingly, patterns of taste dictated by purely commercial considerations win acceptance, and the natural feeling for quality and appropriateness is dissipated in the giddy tumble from novelty to novelty. The individual is so dazed by the profusion of goods which merchandising propagandists press upon him that he no longer retains much personal initiative or sales resistance.

From "The Curse of Conformity" by Walter Gropius, in *Adventures of the Mind,* Thruelson and Kobler, editors. Vintage Books.

CONCLUSION: ______________________________

____

____

____

REASONS: ______________________________

____

____

____

____

____

5. *"In this age of scientific achievement, we can overcome any difficulties caused by population growth. If necessary, we could find new sources of food and migrate to other planets."*

We have come to expect great things from the laboratories, but we had better not stretch our luck. The population explosion is happening right now, and will get worse every year. Meanwhile the United States, with its best efforts and after many embarrassing delays, has succeeded in putting only a few men briefly into orbit. To talk about our fledgling space instruments as a means of solving a *current* problem is not only absurd; it is irresponsible. To think of space vehicles as solving future problems is hardly more reassuring. Presumably none of us would be delighted at the prospect of living on Venus, for instance, in temperatures hundreds of degrees above boiling, or on the moon, in temperatures hundreds of degrees below zero.

In short, scientific panaceas—the attractive visions of widespread solar and atomic power, civilian space travel, plentiful and palatable food from new sources, and so on—are still too far in the future to be practicably relevant to the present population problem. It is no help to people who are hungry *now* to advise them that "We'll fix everything tomorrow."

From *The Silent Explosion* by Philip Appleman. Copyright ©1964. Reprinted by permission of Beacon Press.

CONCLUSION: ______________________________

____

____

____

REASONS: ______________________________

____

____

____

____

____

6. Man can learn to tolerate treeless avenues, starless skies, tasteless food, a monotonous succession of holidays which have become spiritless and meaningless because they are no longer holy days, a life without the fragrance of flowers, the song of birds, the joyous intoxication of spring, or the melancholy of autumn. Loss of the amenities of life may have no obvious detrimental effect on man's physical well-being or on his ability to per-

form effectively as part of the economic or technological machine. Increasingly, in fact, most professional activities are carried on in denatured dwellings, offices, and industrial plants. The popularity of the Los Angeles airport for important meetings has already been mentioned. Schools for young children are being built underground to facilitate the upkeep of rooms and lessen distractions for the pupils!

Little if anything is known, however, of the ultimate effect on man of such drastic elimination of the natural stimuli under which he has evolved as a biological being. Air, water, soil, and fire, the rhythms of nature and the variety of living things, are not of interest only as chemical mixtures, physical forces, or biological phenomena: they are the very influences that have shaped human life and thereby created deep human needs that will not change in the foreseeable future. The pathetic weekend exodus to the country or beaches, the fireplaces in overheated city apartments, testify to the persistence in man of biological and emotional hungers that developed during his evolutionary past, and that he cannot outgrow.

Man will continue searching for significance by relating himself to other men, and to the totality of the universe that he may identify with God. But while pursuing significance outside of himself he should not forget that he is still of the earth. Like Antaeus of the Greek legend, he loses his strength when both his feet are off the ground.

CONCLUSION: ______________________________

____

____

____

REASONS: ______________________________

____

____

____

____

____

7. A wise democratic government will certainly absorb the most popular ideas of the opposition and often incorporate them into its own program, much to the dismay of its political opponent. In the history of the American and British democracies we find many instances of this kind of adoption of new ideas. The third parties, the reform movements at the turn of the century, Norman Thomas and his socialists in the United States, and the Liberals of Great Britain—all of these almost exclusively fulfilled the function of originating ideas. It is only natural that such a way of forestalling constructive criticism and the resulting increase in staying power for the government brings much disappointment and bitterness to the opposition awaiting its turn. In the Western countries, the great expansion of the powers of the governing party and its self-proclaimed identification with the state we have witnessed in recent years certainly justify some concern, since such a situation may lead to the weakening of the political initiative and responsibility of the opposition. For it is undoubtedly an important responsiblity of the governing party—even though it may not be a virtue that comes easily—not to drive the opposition into hopeless apathy but to grant the political opponent an appropriate position. The vitality of democracy depends in no small measure on the presence of constructive alternatives in the system.

From *Democracy in a Changing Society,* Henry W. Ehrmann, editor. Frederick A. Praeger, Publishers.

CONCLUSION: ______________________________

____

____

____

REASONS: ______________________________

____

____

8. It's the season for touring national parks—and for park managers and conservationists to decry the neglect of the "crown jewels" like Yellowstone. On the strength of a tour of Mesa Verde, Zion and Bryce and the north rim of the Grand Canyon, let me file a brief for protecting the parks at all reasonable cost.

Discussions of the budget and morale of the National Park Service are boring only to those who have never set foot inside their preserve. But those living far from the celebrated Rocky Mountain parks also have a stake in the service; Eastern parks like the Cape Cod National Seashore and New York's Gateway rank near the top in annual attendance.

Much of America's cultural history as well as geology is encased in the national parks. Mesa Verde, for example, features an incomparable neighborhood preservation program—the cliff dwellings built eight centuries ago by the Anasazi ancestors of the Pueblo Indians.

In any case, the awesome spectacles and serene pleasures of the national parks are no secret to millions of Americans. That's the problem. Attendance has quadrupled in 20 years. Their acreage has been expanded but their appropriations have been held in check. Conservationists say that park maintenance has suffered in many places and that older facilities, like Yellowstone's Old Faithful Inn, built in 1903 of fir and lodgepole pine, are firetraps. Park rangers, who once thought of themselves as guides and naturalists, now function much of the time as policemen, and even carry pistols.

Still, the neglect is not universal. The four parks I visited seemed to be well cared for and able to cope with the crowds. The clamor for more money ought not to obscure the fact that many parks, perhaps even most, are not overburdened.

But the risks of overcrowding are obvious. Only a few dozen visitors can fit into Mesa Verde's Balcony House, one of the Indian cliff dwellings. An overload would endanger both the sure-footed sightseers and the sight. We sweltered in line for 90 minutes while waiting our turn. The meadows at Maroon Bells in the White River National Forest outside of Aspen, Colo., are awash with wild flowers. Crowds that ignore the paths or overflow them could trample this treasure. Some populists oppose all entry restrictions to public parks but for both automobiles and people, they are sometimes the only way to prevent destruction.

Balancing the budget priorities and reconciling public rights and park preservation are vexing problems now. They become harder every year. Will the national parks become monuments to neglect, like New York's subways or the pockmarked interstate turnpikes that sorely taxed my shock absorbers? I hope not. The crown jewels and other gems of the park system are precious to the nation's past and future. Their claim on the national budget is very special.

CONCLUSION: ______________________________

REASONS: ______________________________

9. We are all born with potentialities for speech, but whether we will speak at all is dependent entirely upon the kind of exposure we receive to speaking human beings. As children, if we only hear a word now and again and are not involved in the necessity of learning the meaning of things, the probabilities are high that we will never speak. Some years ago in Ohio a little girl was found locked up in a closet where she had been kept for five years with her deaf-mute mother. At the age of five years when she was discovered or liberated, this little girl could not utter a word, but after some six months of intensive work with a speech expert she eventually learned to speak perfectly. She had, incidentally, received a great deal of love from her deaf-mute mother during their incarceration None of us would ever speak unless we heard other people speak-

ing. We possess the general potentialities for speech, but what language we will speak will depend entirely upon the language we hear spoken. And so it is with all our behavioral potentialities. How we will behave about them depends largely upon the manner in which we have been taught by the environment around us. Our very senses have to be taught in this way. Our tactile sense, how we see, hear—all these we have to learn.

From *Human Heredity* by Ashley Montague. Reprinted by permission of The New American Library.

CONCLUSION: ____

____

____

REASONS: ____

____

____

____

____

____

10. How could anyone expect good teamwork, group loyalty or a common interest in raising firm productivity when almost half of the work force will either quit or be laid off within twelve months? Neither worker nor company has any interest in the economic success of the other. Workers, including managers, are not willing to sacrifice to help build the future prosperity of the company since they know that they will not be around to share in that future prosperity. Conversely the company is not willing to invest in the future success of the individual since that person is apt to be somewhere else when the investment that goes into training him pays off.

The result is gross underinvestment in creating the on-the-job skills necessary for industrial success. Blue-collar workers are traditionally trained on the job, but with today's high turnover rates no firm wants to invest in training its work force since there is a very high probability that the workers will soon leave for another job. For each firm it is cheaper to bid, with higher wages, a skilled worker away from other firms, but this obviously does not work for the economy as a whole. The result is a perpetual shortage of skilled blue-collar workers whenever the economy begins to approach anything remotely resembling full employment.

The problem is visible in foreign trade. To be a successful exporter it is necessary to speak the languages of the countries to which you wish to sell your products. Foreign firms are willing to pay to teach their employees the languages that they need to be salesmen abroad. American firms generally are not. The differences show how long they expect their employees to remain on the payroll.

The American corporation is accused of having a short-run time horizon. But if everyone, workers and managers, is basically on his own when it comes to economic success, how could anyone expect the American corporation to have a long time horizon? If each individual foresees that he will be with the firm for only a brief period, then it should come as no surprise that the corporation has an equally short time horizon in its planning.

Job hopping is only part of the problem of excessive employee turnover. U.S. firms are also quicker to fire workers in cyclical economic downturns than are their foreign counterparts. Compare the behavior of Chrysler and Mazda when they both faced economic extinction. Chrysler fired thousands of workers; Mazda went to great lengths to keep employees with the company. If firms fire workers when it is economically convenient, no one should be surprised when American workers abandon their firms when it is economically convenient.

To increase training, strengthen teamwork and lengthen time horizons, American corporations are going to have to adopt management practices that dramatically cut turnover rates. If America wants a loyal labor force interested in raising productivity, layoffs have to become the last, rather than the first, resort when a firm is facing difficult economic times. Incentives will have to be structured to give the biggest economic prizes to those who do not job hop. "Every man for himself" is not the route to economic success.

From "A Plague of Job Hoppers." Reprinted by permission from *Time*.

CONCLUSION: ____

____

REASONS: ______________________________